Dedicated to my wife, Rachel
and my son, Judah

HOW THIS BOOK WORKS

Each chord in this book has both a picture and a graphic. The graphic
is a representation of your guitar neck as if you were looking straight
at it. Hold out your guitar (facing you) to see the same angle.

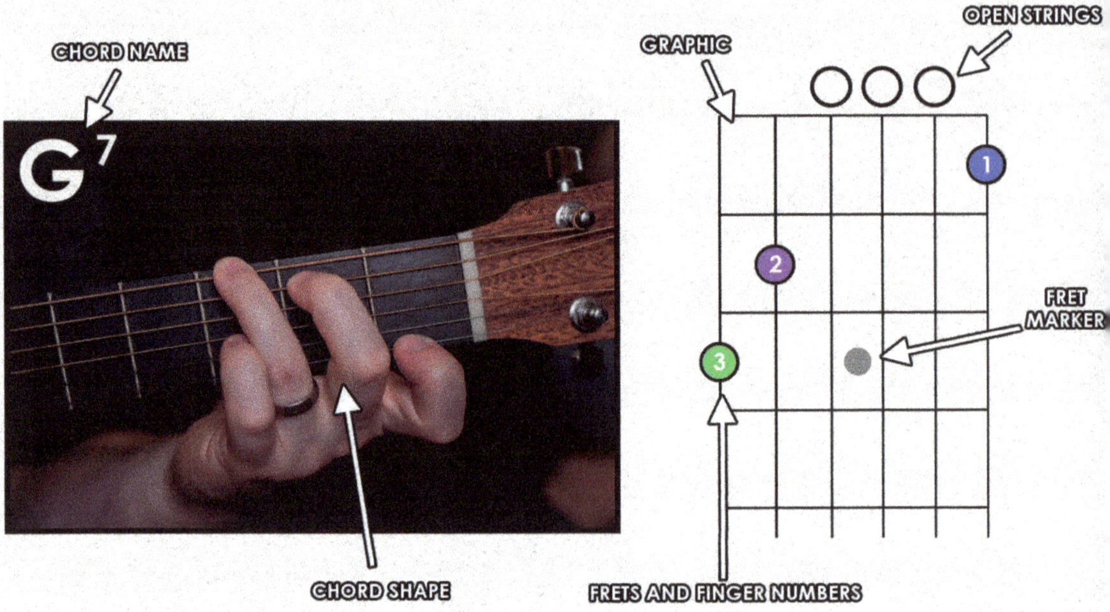

The chord name is in the top left of every picture.
On the graphic, we have some circles that are hollow and some that
are filled in with color and a number.

The hollow circles are open strings (no frets need to be pressed down).
The circles with colors show us where we need to place our fingers.
The number is which finger we're going to use to press that fret.

There are two things to keep an eye on:

Firstly, if you see the same finger number multiple times in a single chord
know that we are dealing with a bar chord.

Secondly, keep an eye on the fret markers (gray dots in the middle).
Not every chord starts in the same place on the fretboard. Mark where
these are on your own guitar, and watch where they fall in this book.

If we do play a chord higher on the neck that needs to start from a specific
fret, we will mark that out with a small number next to the chord graphic.

Happy playing!

OPEN CHORDS

Our first group of chords are open chords. These types of chords are played on the lower-numbered frets, and are broken up into major, minor and 7 chords.

When we talk about chords we often number the notes we're using, starting with the first note in the chord. For exampe, when we're playing a G chord we can number the letters in the musical alphabet starting with a G note:

G	A	B	C	D	E	F	G
1	2	3	4	5	6	7	1

Our open chords utilize notes 1 - 3 and 5. In our example of a G chord, these would be notes G - B and D:

G	A	B	C	D	E	F	G
1	2	3	4	5	6	7	1

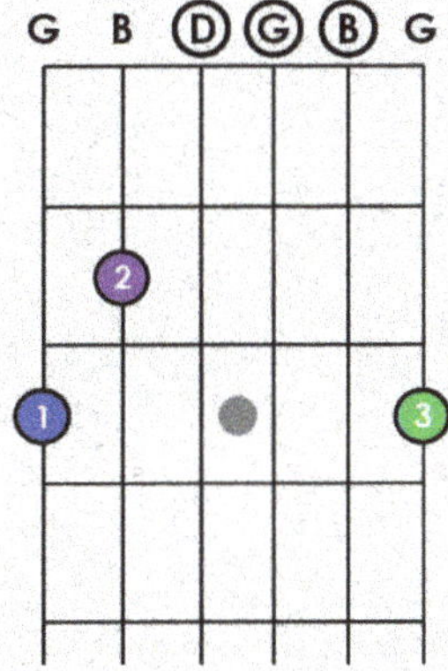

The exception is the 7 chord, which uses the 7th note as well, and so has 4 unique notes:

G	A	B	C	D	E	F	G
1	2	3	4	5	6	7	1

A

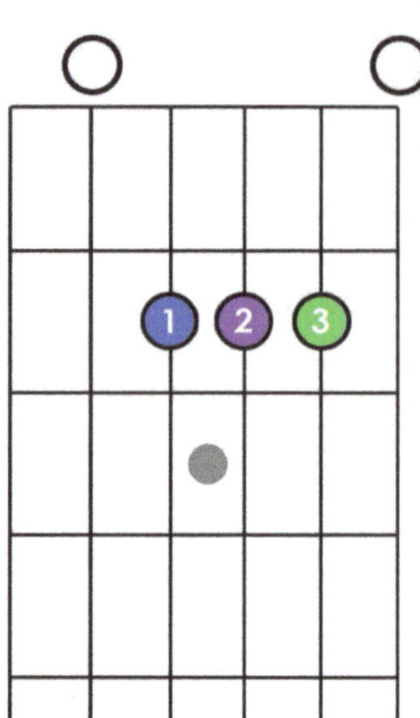

A^m

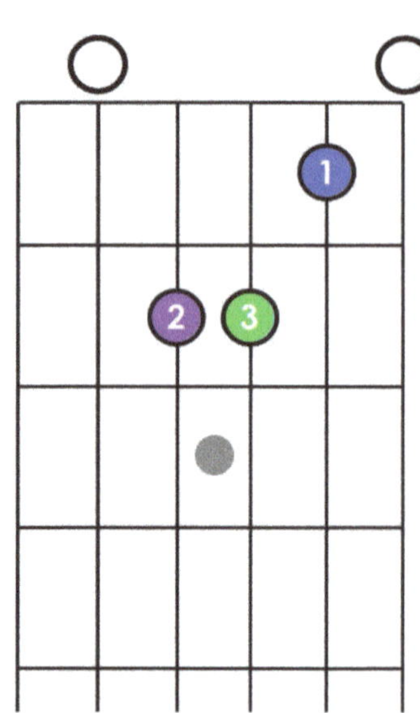

A^7

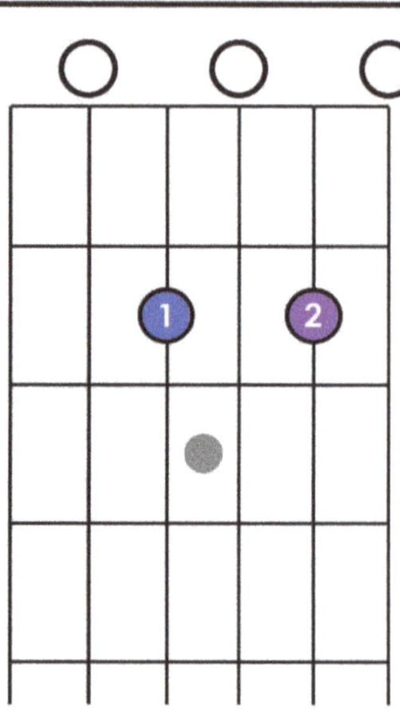

B

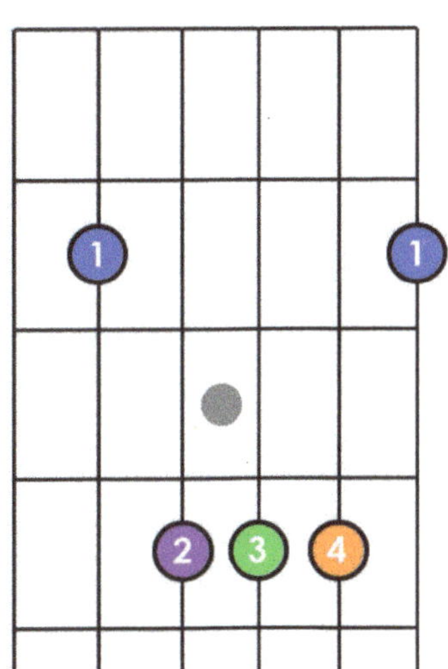

B^m

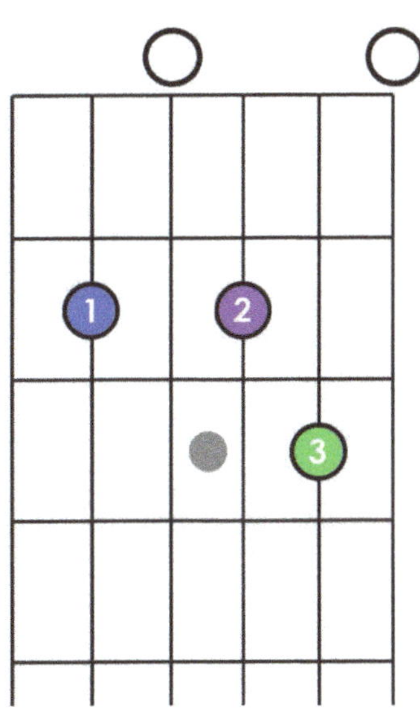

B⁷

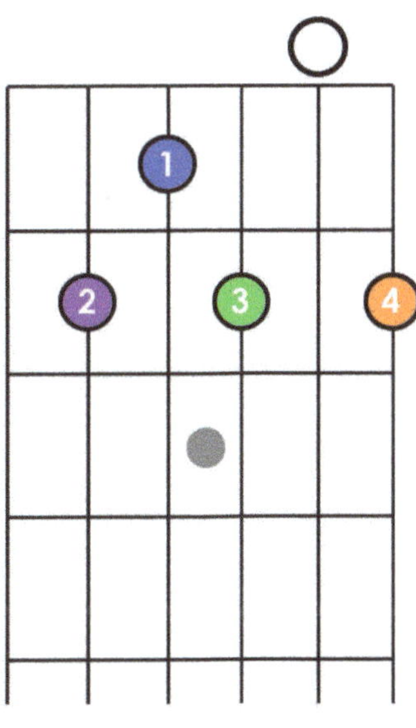

C

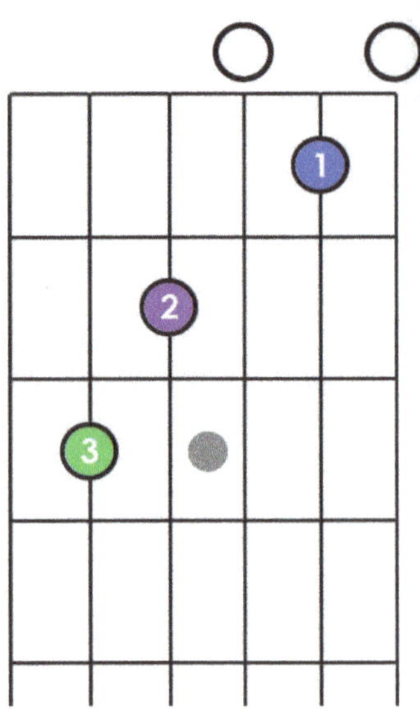

Cm

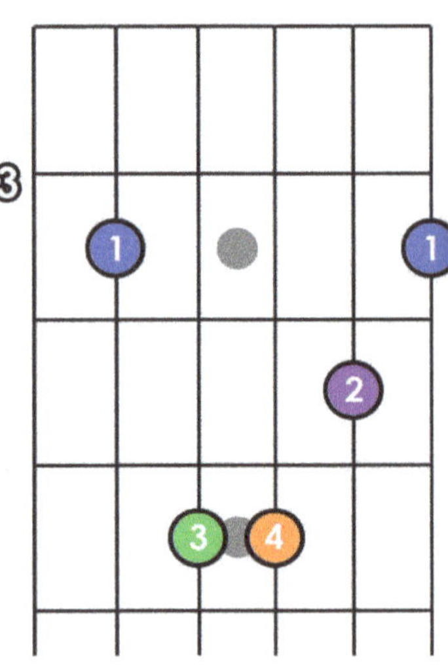
3

C7

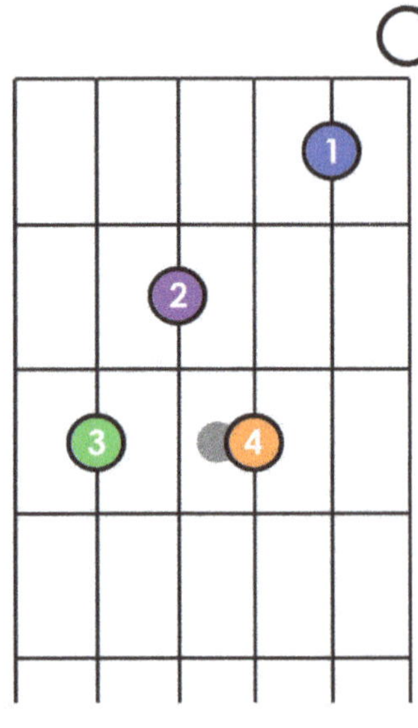

D

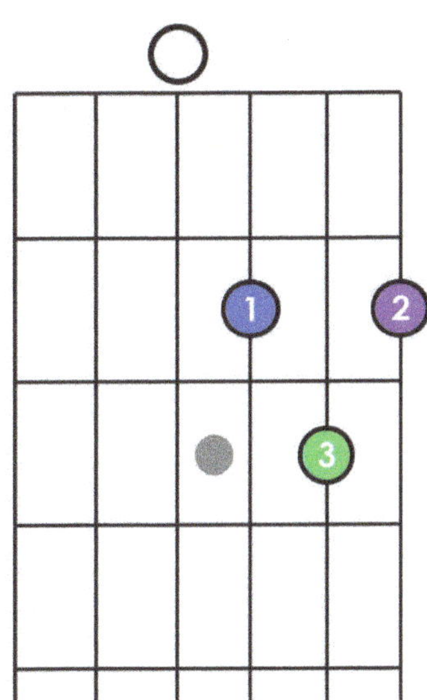

Dm

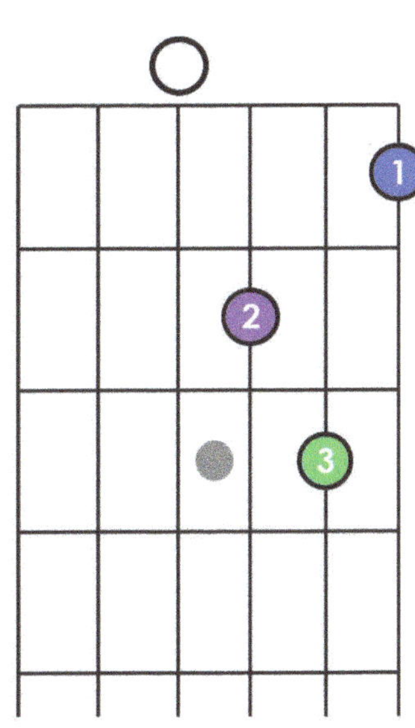

D7

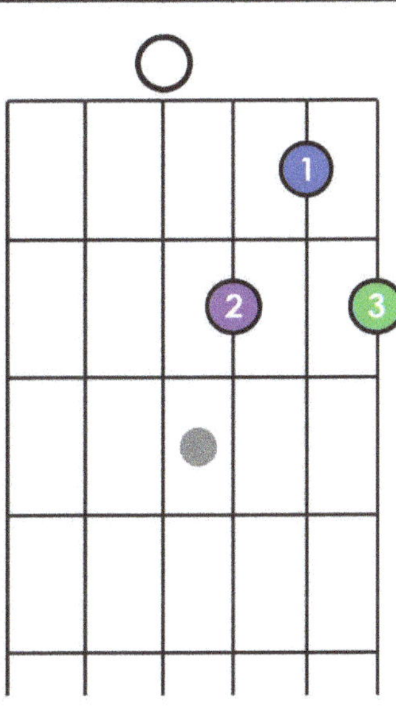

E

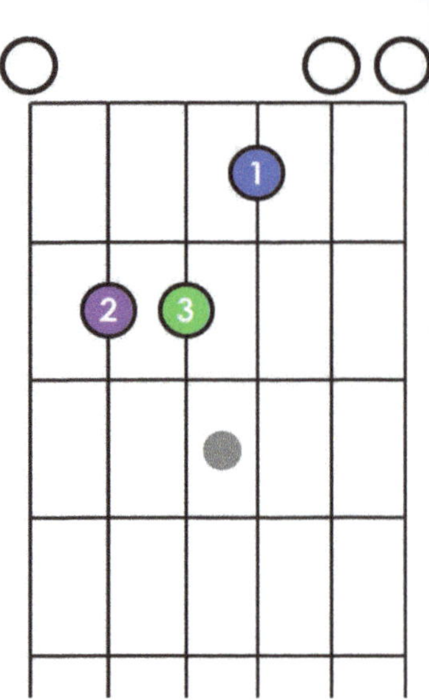

E m

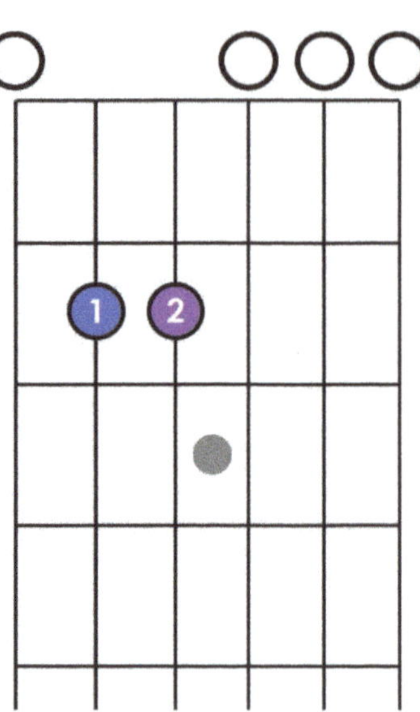

E 7

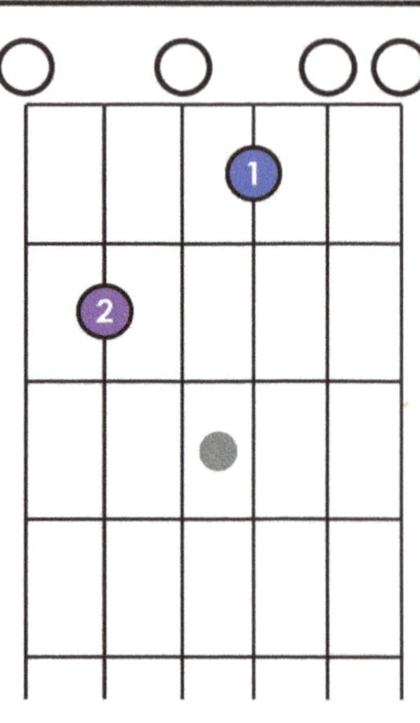

F

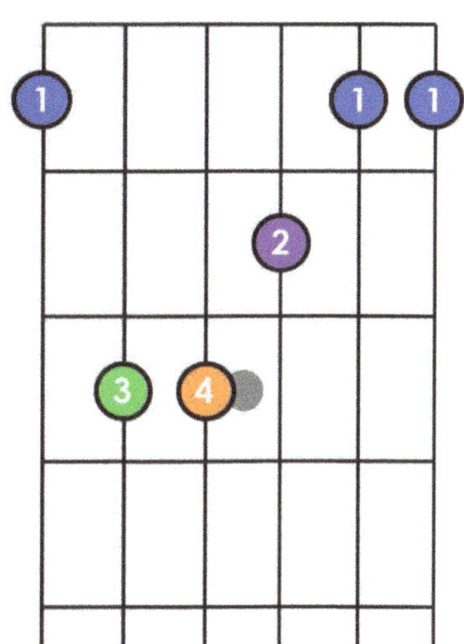

F^m

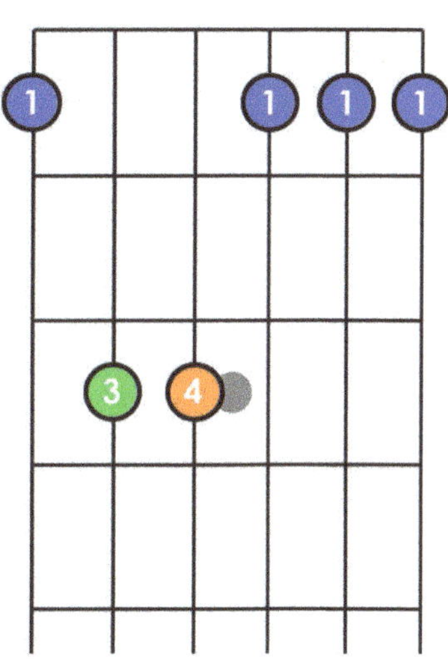

F⁷

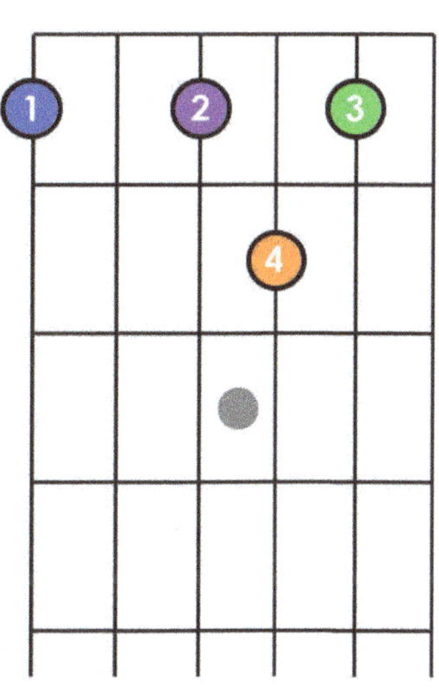

G

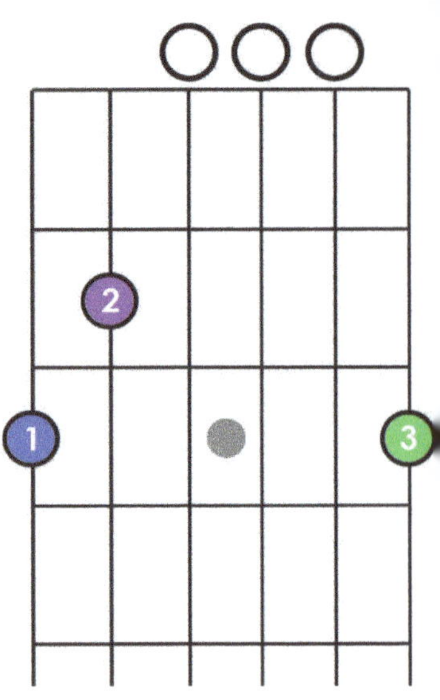

G^m

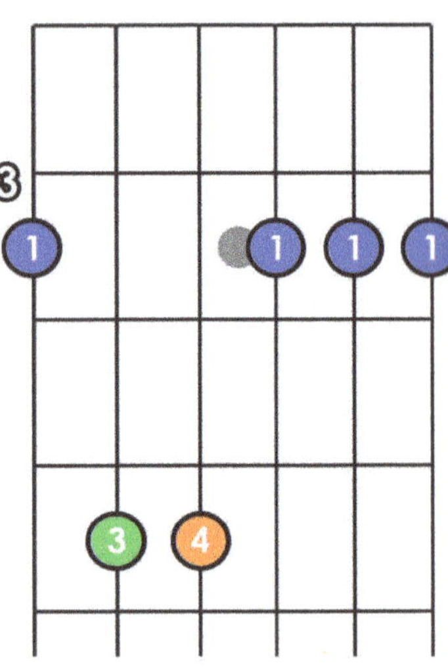

G⁷

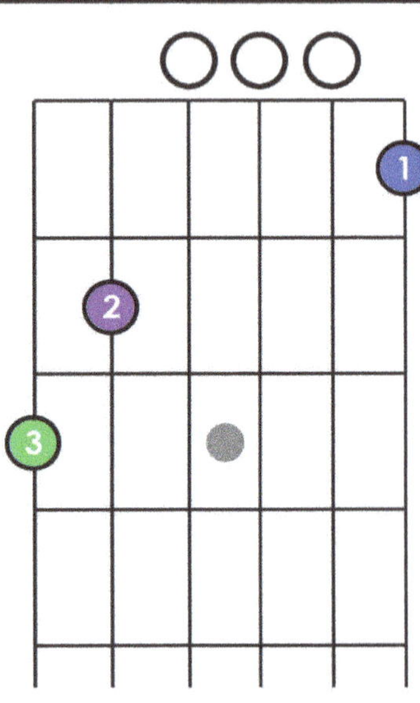

POWER CHORDS

Power chords are a type of chord that are popular in rock and metal music. These are movable shapes that fit all over the neck of the guitar. The position of your power chord should start on the note name that matches what you want your chord to be. For example, we would start a G power chord from a G note.

The power chord shape is the same between the 6th and 5th strings, and works for either major or minor chords. So a G power chord would be exactly the same as a G minor power chord.

Power chords do not use three unique notes like an open chords, but rather play 1 - 5 - 1 (octave):

G	A	B	C	D	E	F	G
1	2	3	4	5	6	7	1

Power Chords

6th String

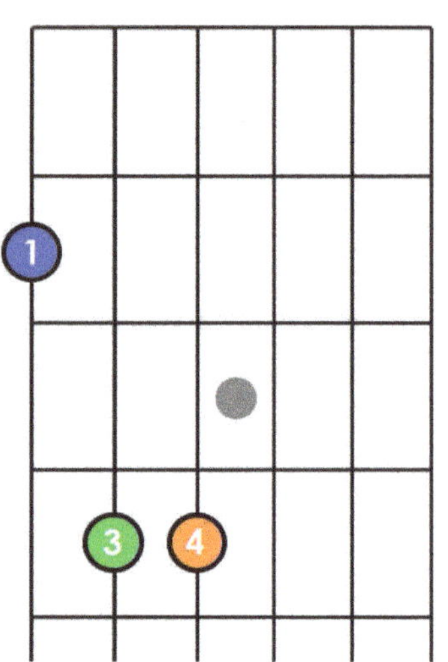

5th String

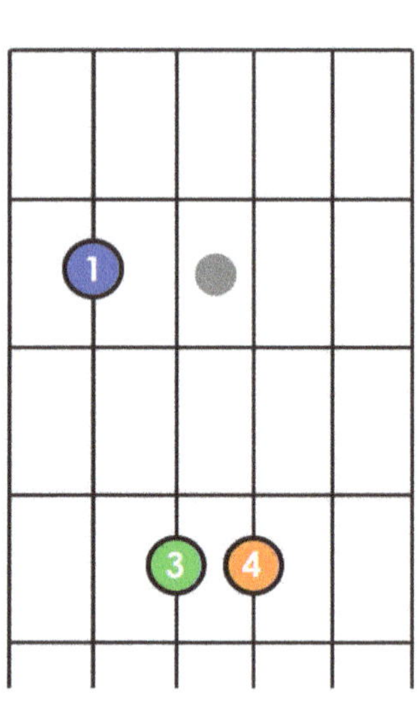

4th String

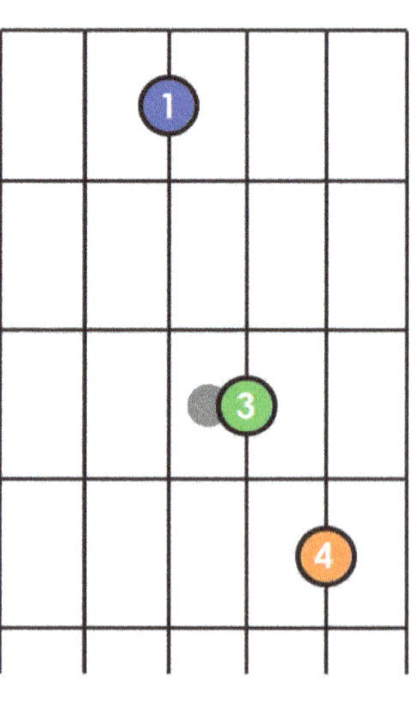

7TH CHORDS

7th chords are our next movable shape that add a hint of jazz or neo-soul to our guitar playing.

There are five types of 7 chords: Major, minor, dominant, half-diminished (also called minor 7 flat 5s), and diminished.

Rather than our number chart, let's relate 7th chords to each other:

<u>**Major:**</u>
1 - 3 - 5 - 7

<u>**Minor:**</u>
1 - b3 - 5 - b7

<u>**Dominant (7):**</u>
1 - 3 - 5 - b7

<u>**Minor 7 (b5):**</u>
1 - b3 - b5 - b7

<u>**Diminished:**</u>
1 - b3 - b5 - bb7

Dominant 7s are the type of 7 we played in our open chords, but they also have a standard shape that is movable around the fretboard.

Major 7 Chords

6th String

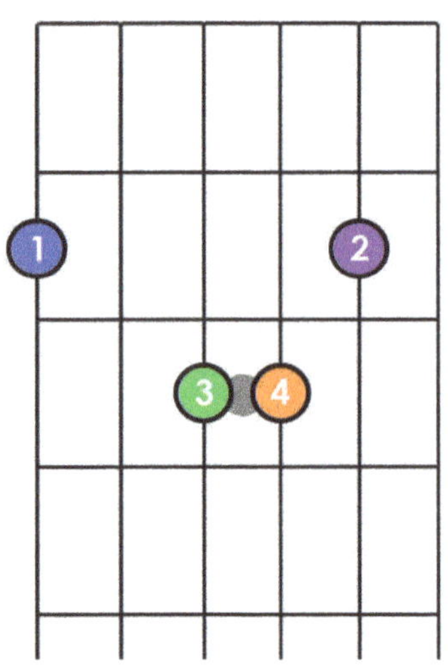

5th String

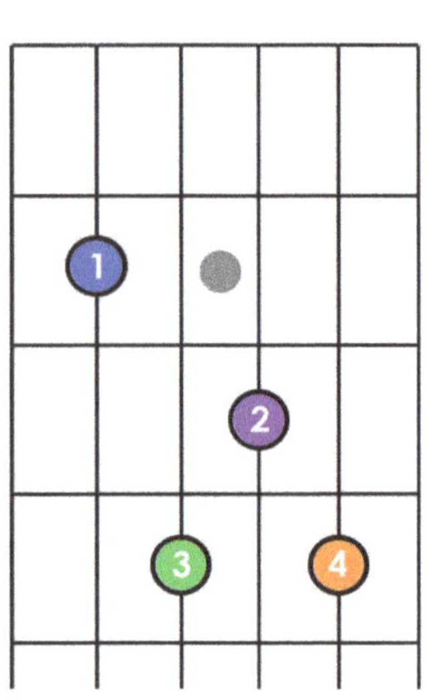

4th String

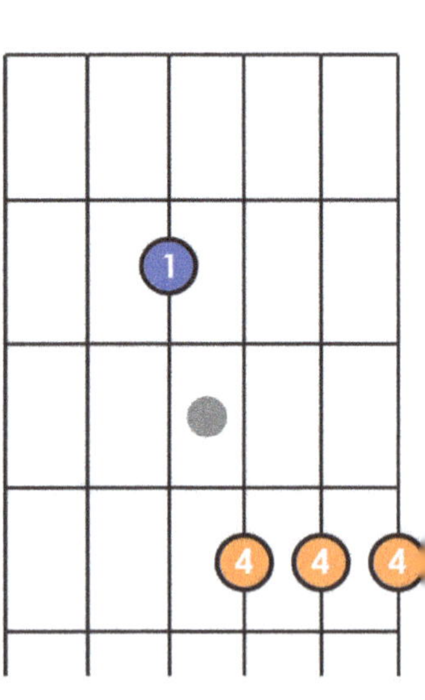

Minor 7 Chords

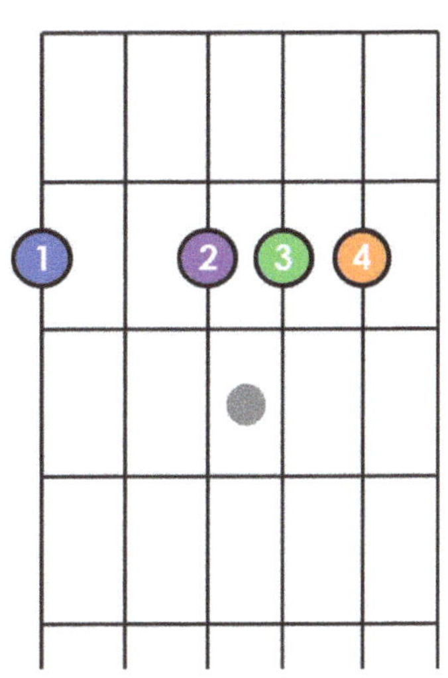

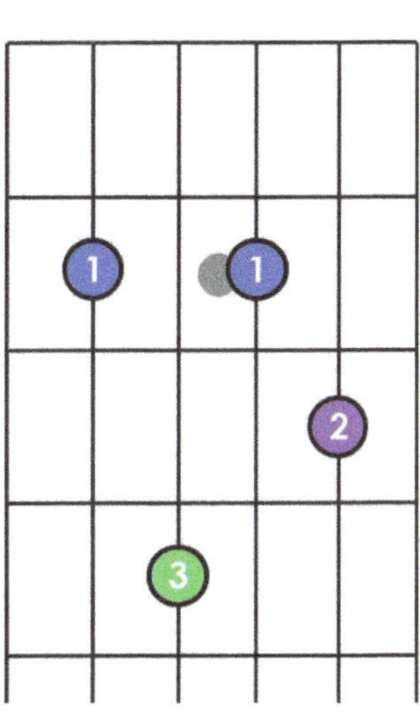

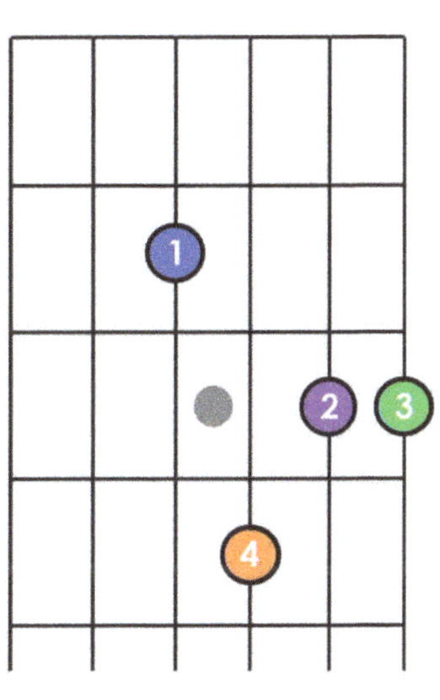

Dominant 7 Chords

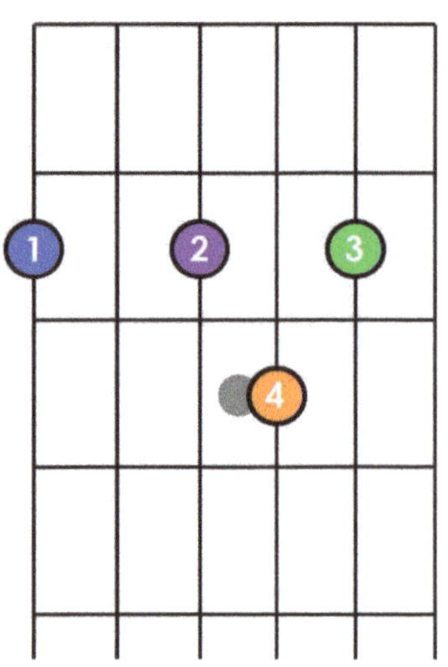

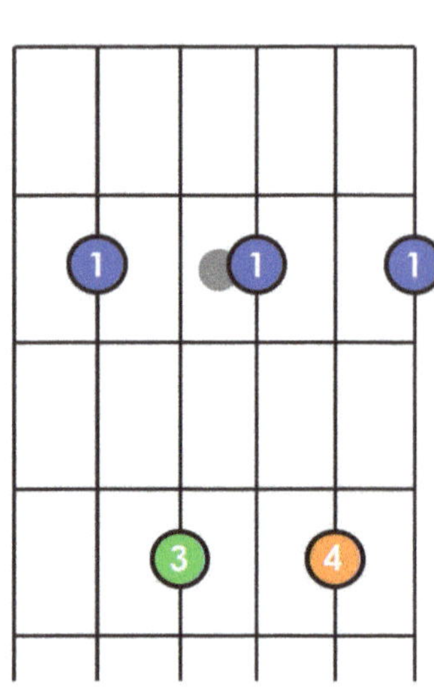

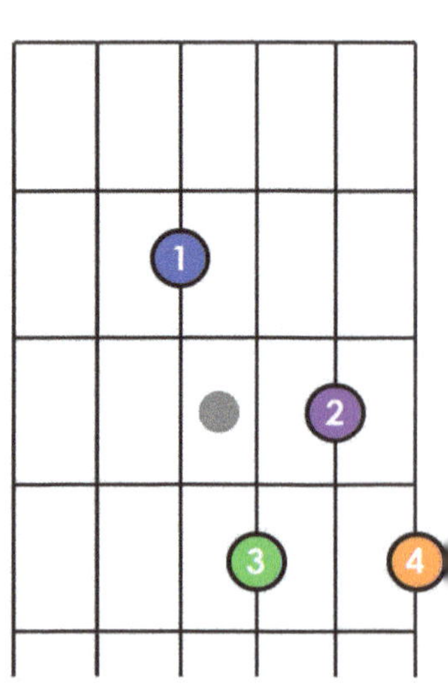

Minor 7$^{(b5)}$ Chords

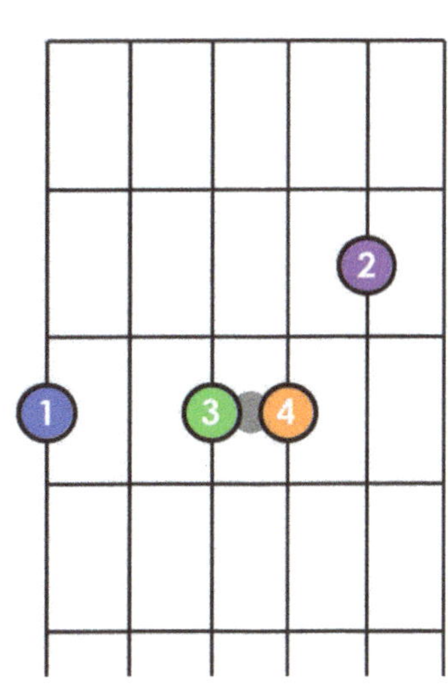

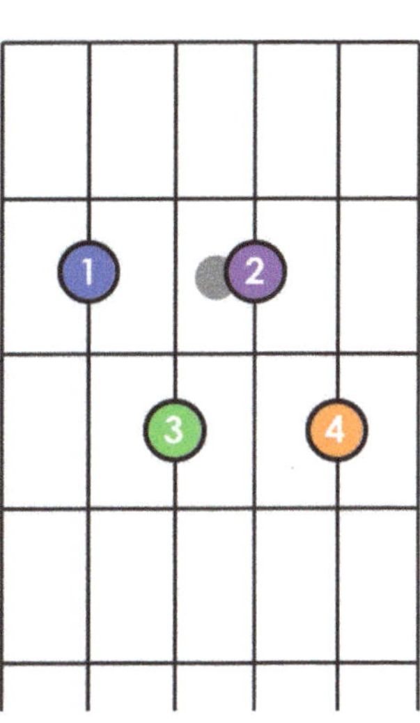

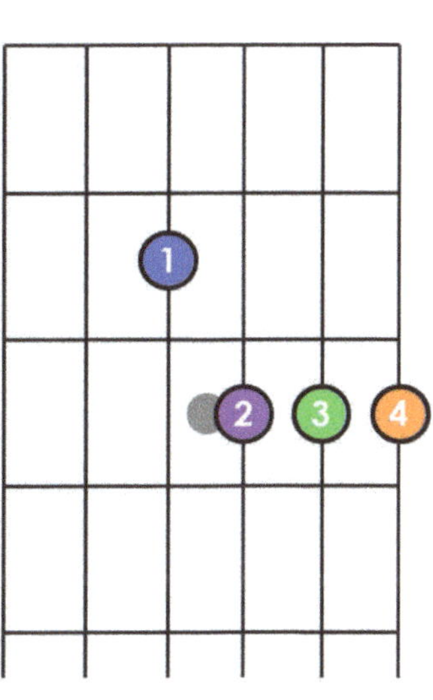

Diminished 7 Chords

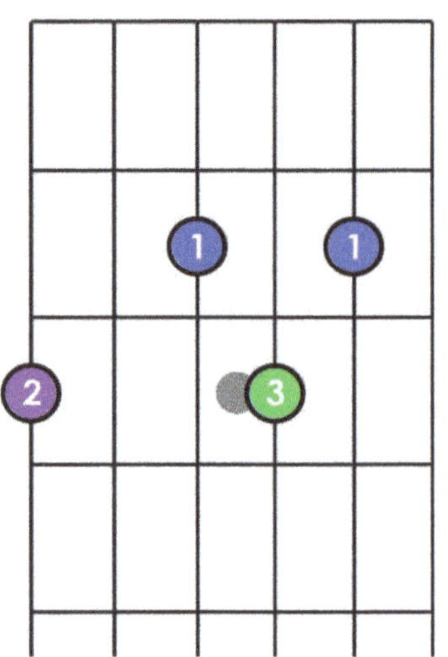

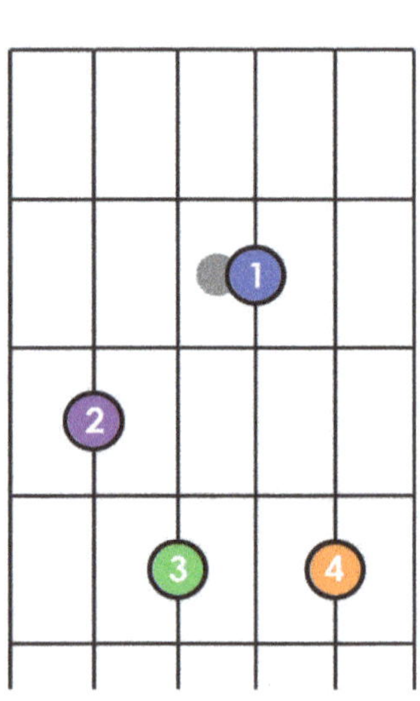

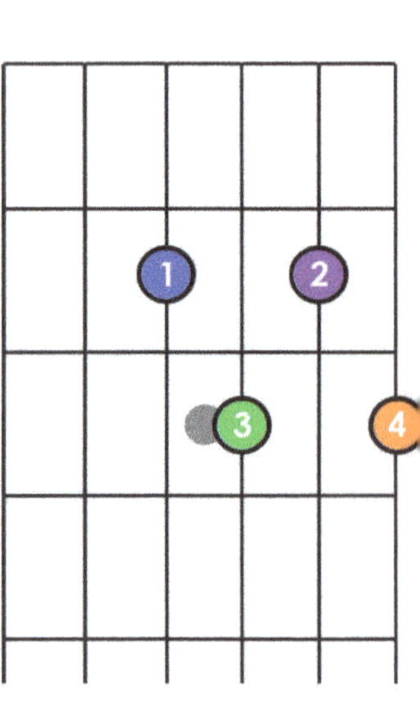

TENSIONS AND EXTENSIONS

Tensions and extensions are notes in chords that add character without adding substance. Primary notes in chords that add substance are 1, 3, 5 and 7.

Tensions are notes that stay within an octave space, while extensions are notes that go beyond the 7th.

For example, a 6th chord has the tension (6) below the octave of the root, so the 6 would be considered a tension:

G	A	B	C	D	E	F	G
1	2	3	4	5	6	7	1

while a 9th chord adds a note beyond the octave - so it would be considered an <u>extension</u>:

G	A	B	C	D	E	F	G	A
1	2	3	4	5	6	7	8	9

Other extensions we'll be covering are 11ths:

G	A	B	C	D	E	F	G	A	B	C
1	2	3	4	5	6	7	8	9	10	11

and 13ths:

G	A	B	C	D	E	F	G	A	B	C	D	E
1	2	3	4	5	6	7	8	9	10	11	12	13

There are two important things we should know about tension and extension chords:

Firstly, not every note is played in longer chords like 11s or 13s. Many of the following shapes that cover those chords pick and choose notes to make a shape.

For example, in our major 13 chord from the 6th string, we play the notes: 1 - 3 - 7 - 13

The second important thing is that extension notes can also have sharp or flat variations. You can make any 9, 11 or 13 note sharp/flat for more interesting (or dissonant) chords.

This works particularly well with dominant chord shapes.

Major 6 Chords

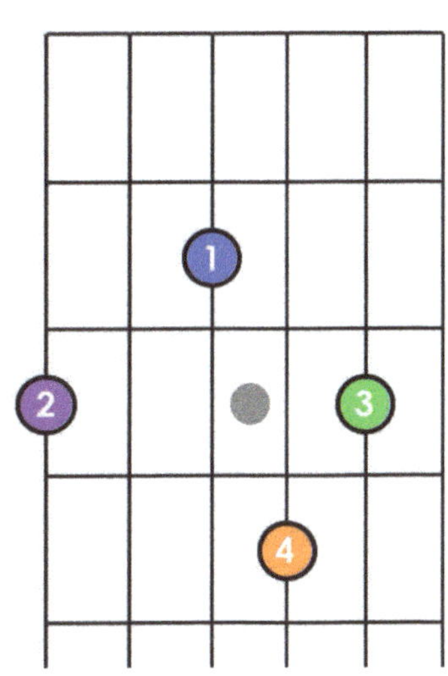

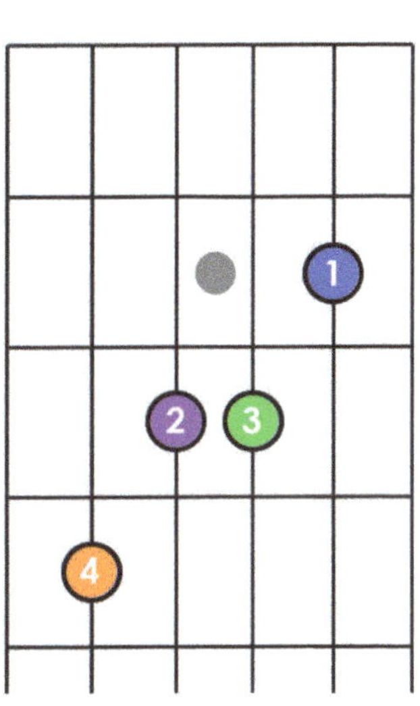

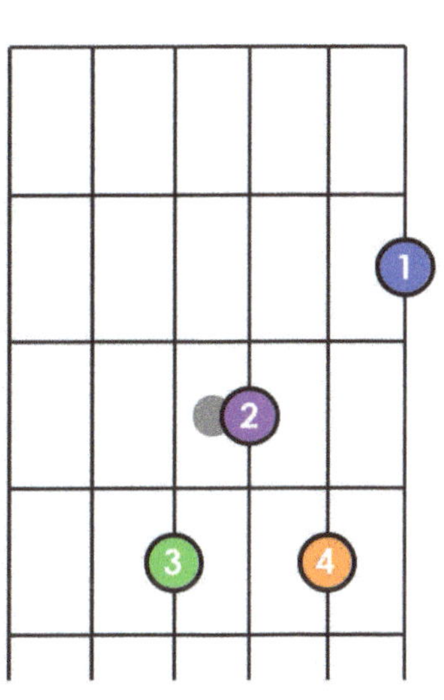

Minor 6 Chords

6th String

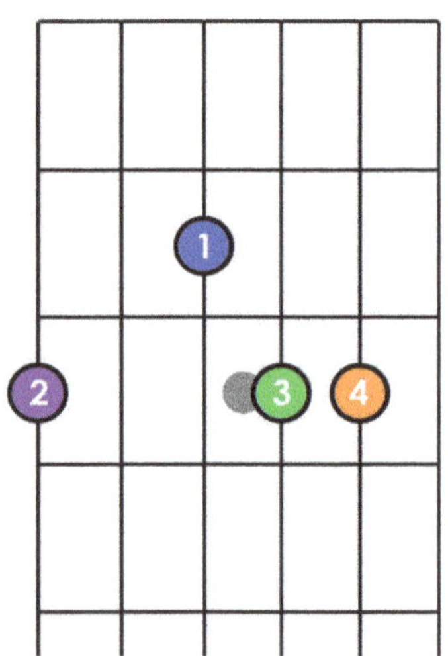

5th String

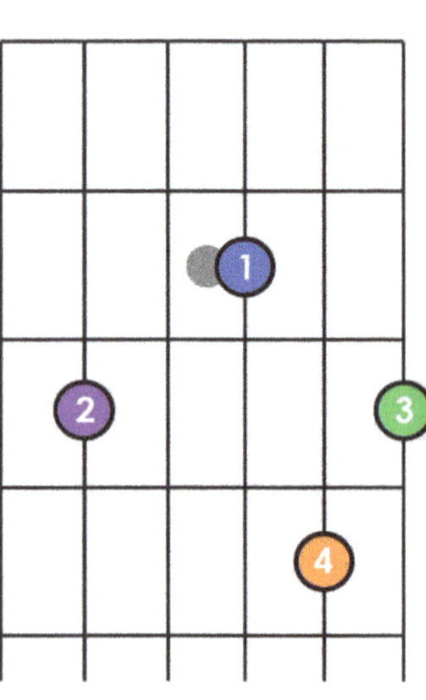

5th String (V)

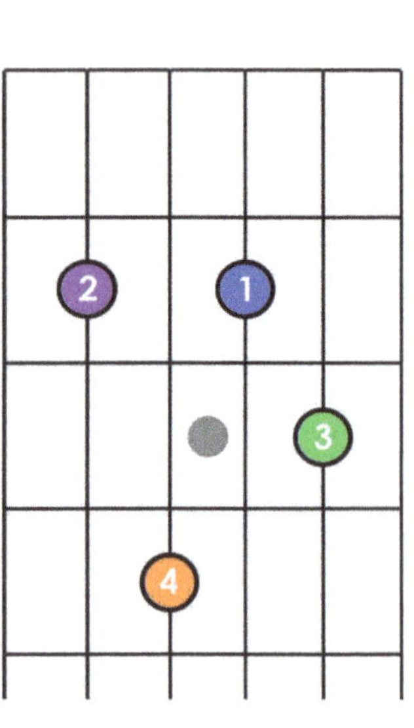

Major 9 Chords

6th String

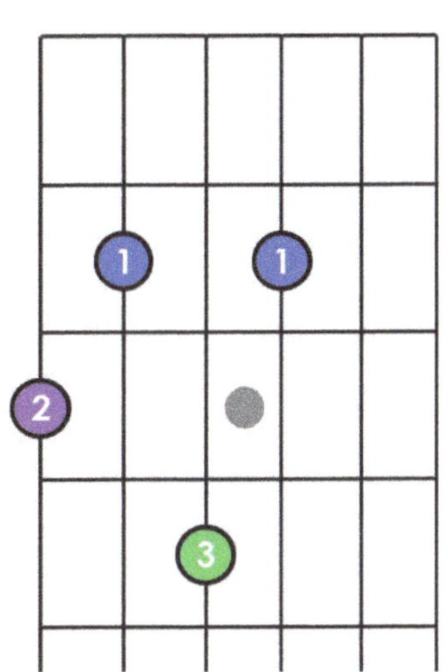

5th String

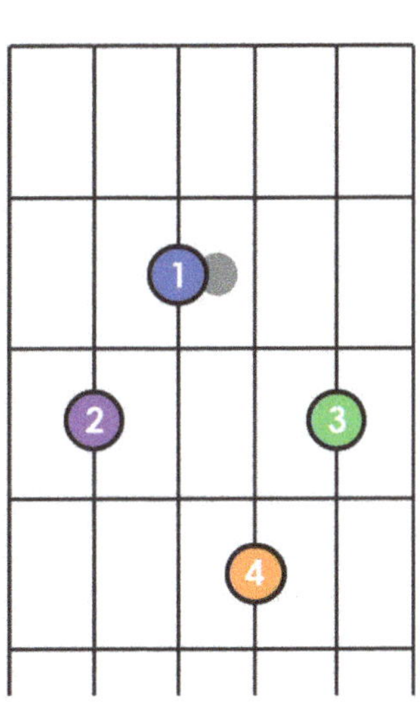

4th String

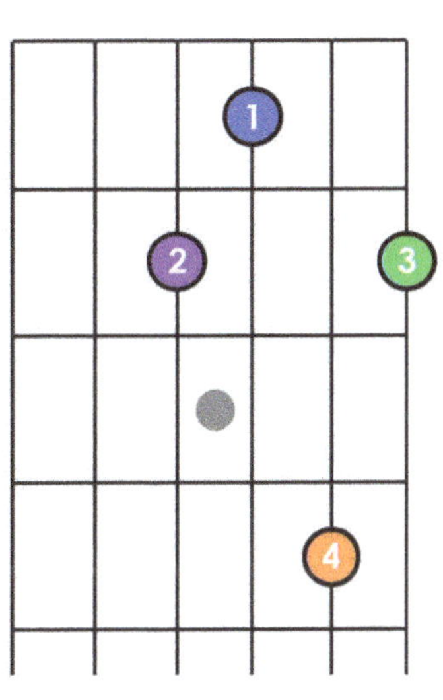

Minor 9 Chords

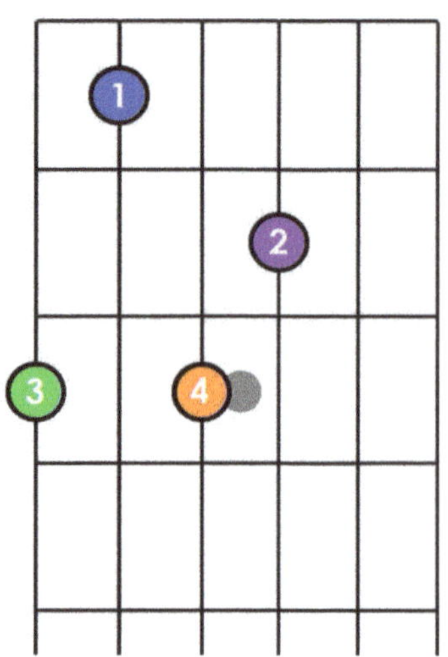

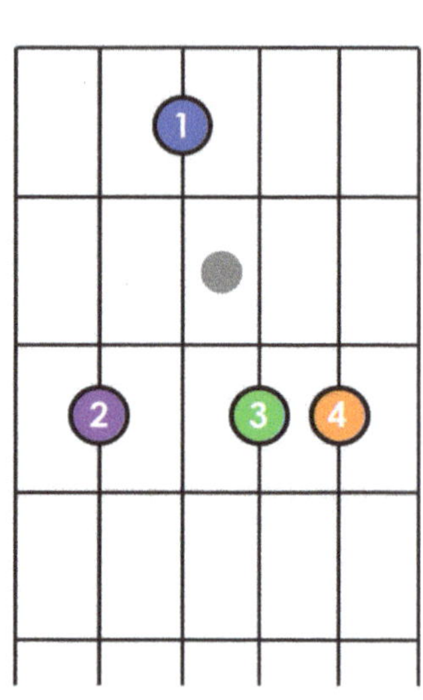

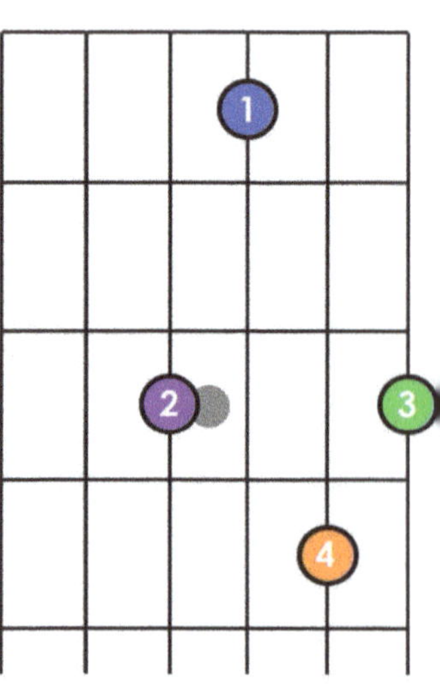

Dominant 9 Chords

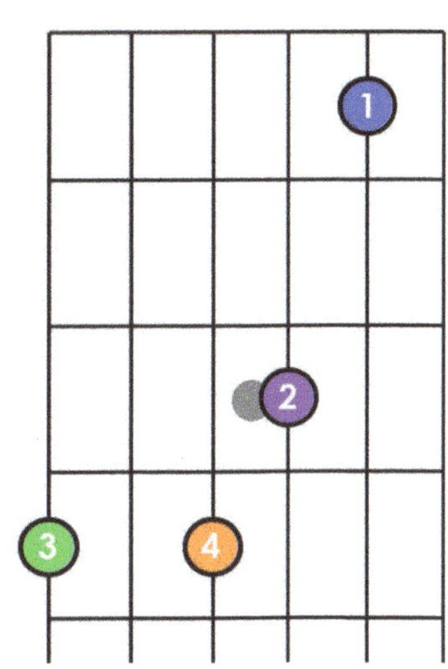

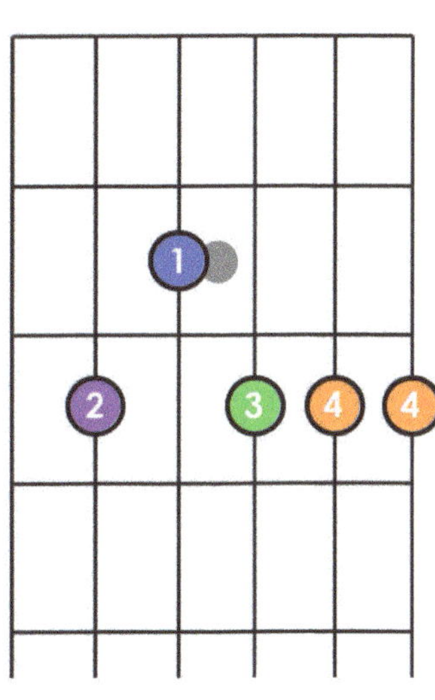

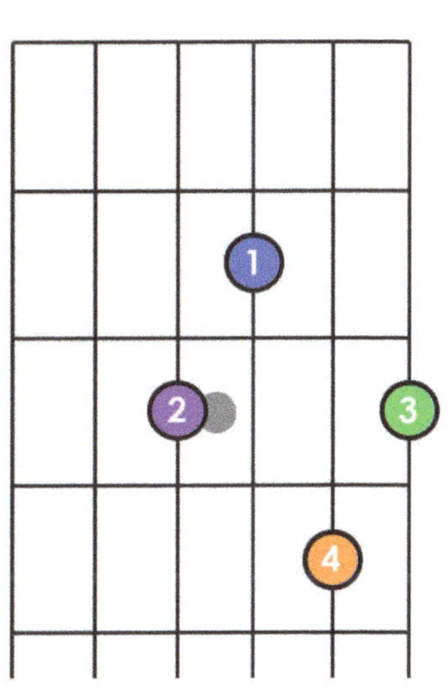

Major 11 Chords

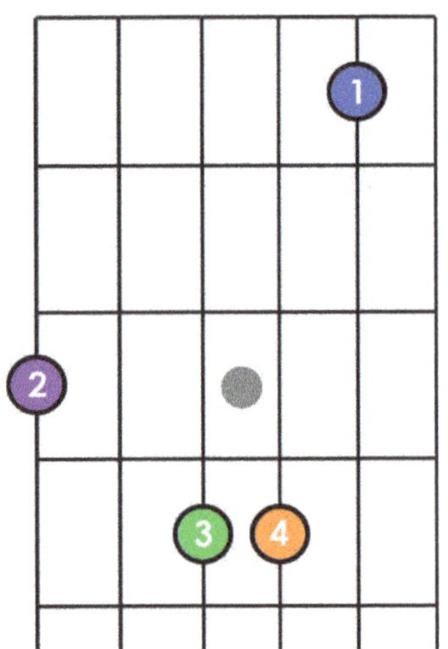

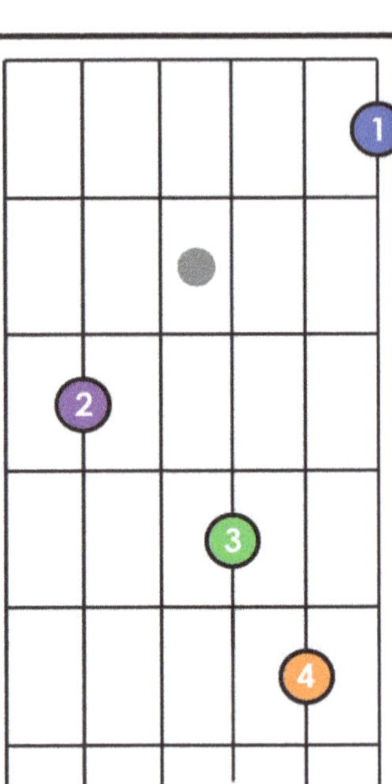

Minor 11 Chords

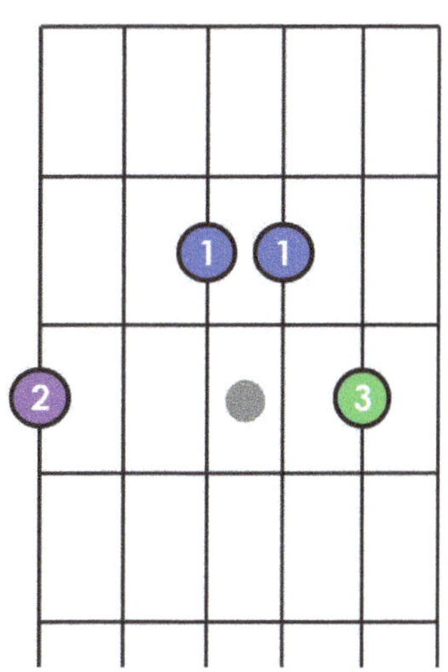

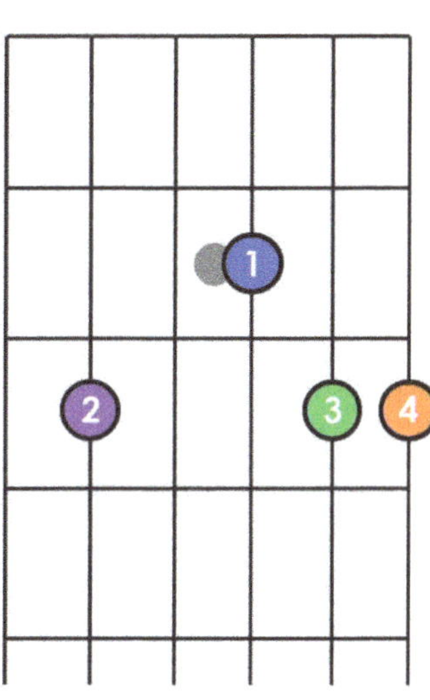

Dominant 11 Chords

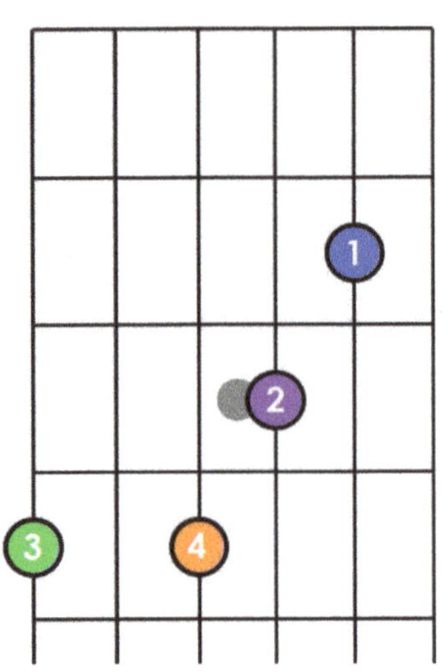

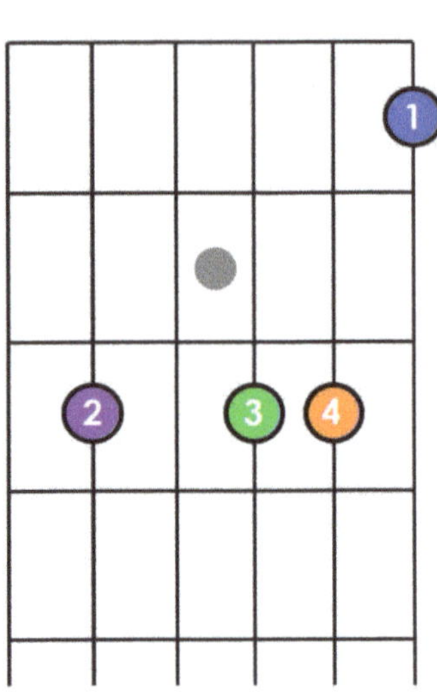

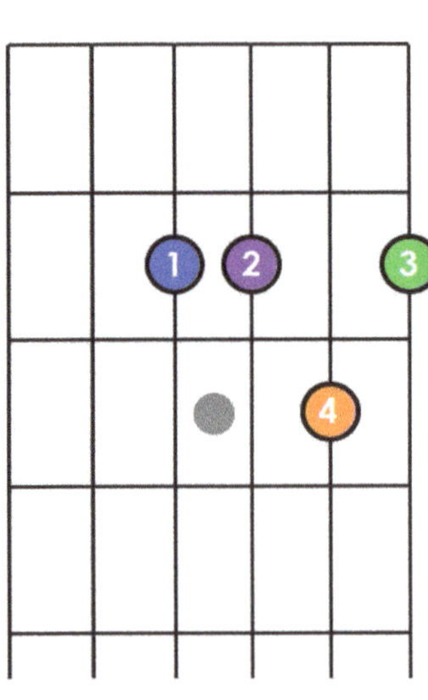

Major 13 Chords

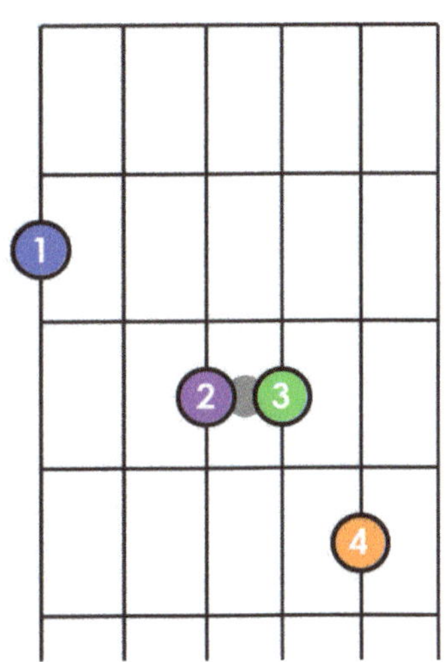

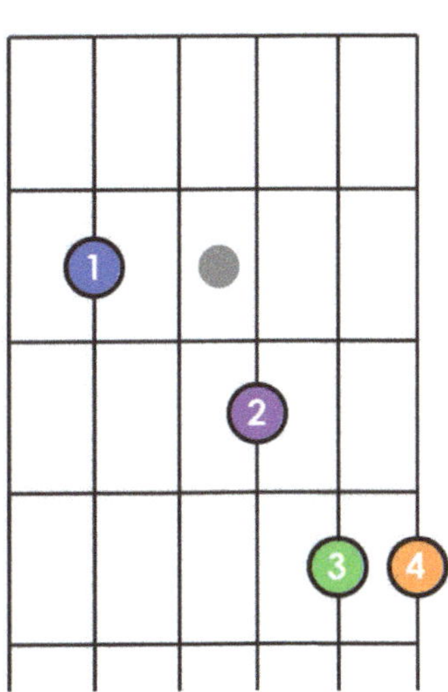

Minor 13 Chords

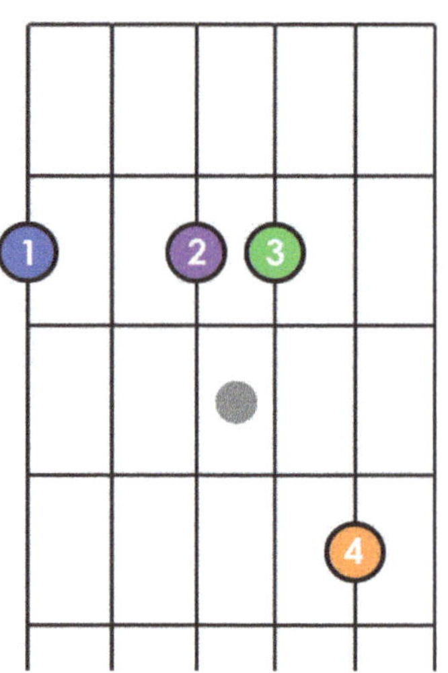

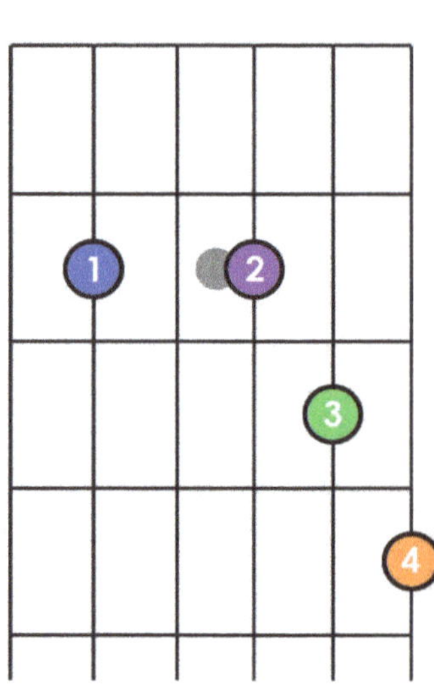

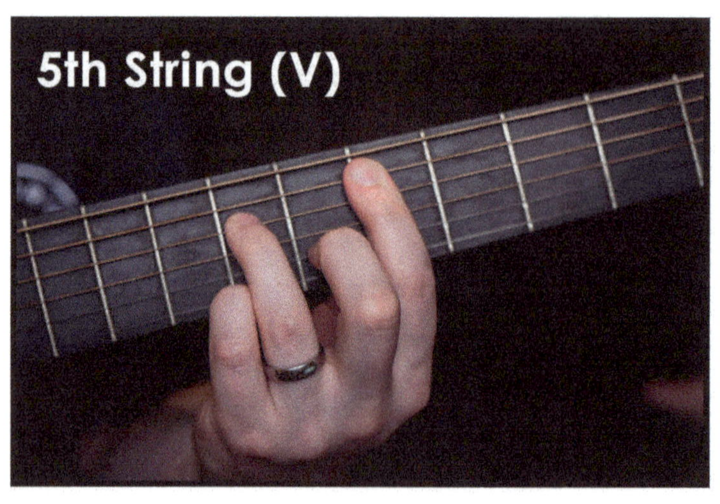

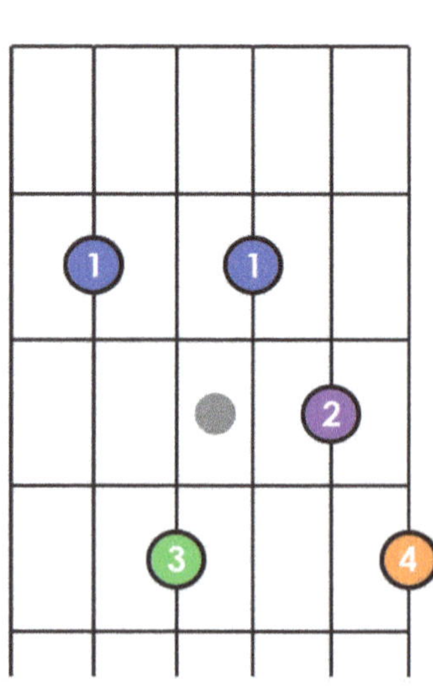

Dominant 13 Chords

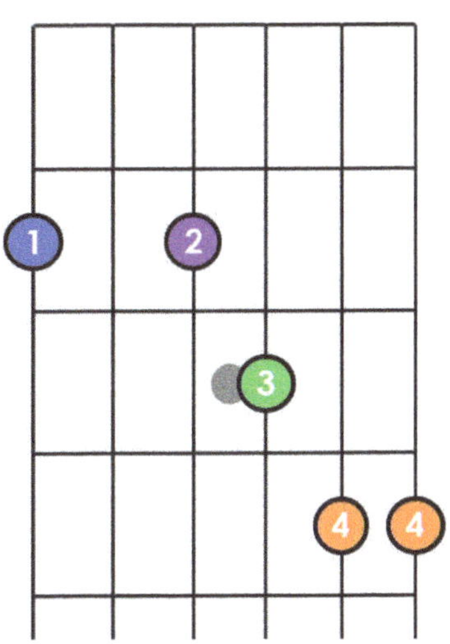

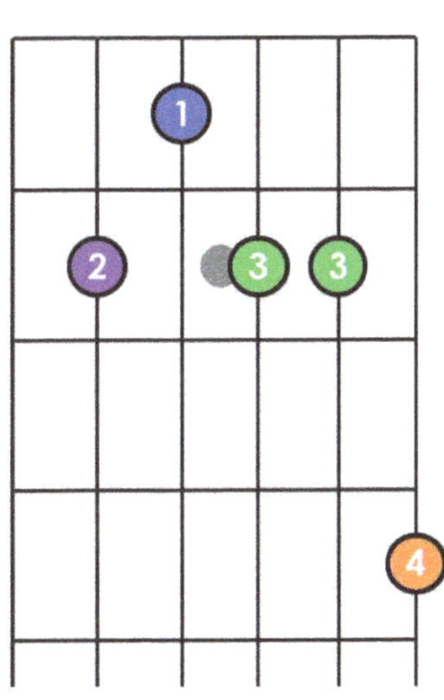

BAR CHORDS

Bar chords (sometimes spelled Barre chords) combine two ideas we've covered so far into one chord. They are both:
notes 1 - 3 - 5 (3 unique notes like our open chords)
and movable shapes (like many other shapes in this book).

Bar chords also have a major, minor and dominant (7) shape just like our open chords.

The difficulty with bar chords is that we need to lay our first finger down across the strings so that it can hold down multiple notes at a time. Many people find this difficult to do when first learning, so don't be tpp hard on yourself! One trick to make these easier is to roll your first finger and bar with the *side* of your finger.

One important thing to notice is that the 4th string versions of bar chords in this book aren't *technically* bar chords, since we aren't barring our finger - but are included in this section to provide a movable shape from the 4th string that would otherwise be omitted.

Major Bar Chords

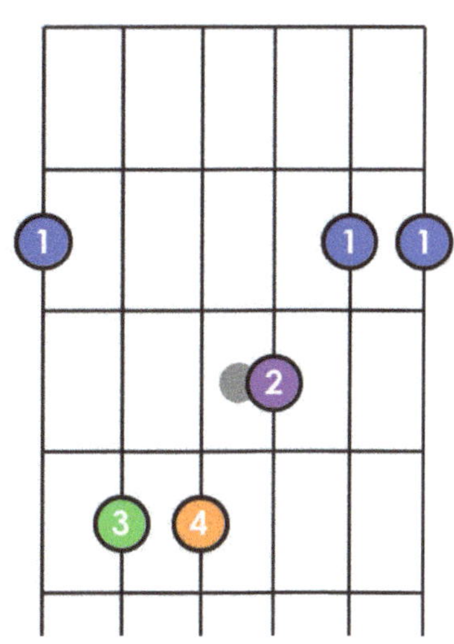

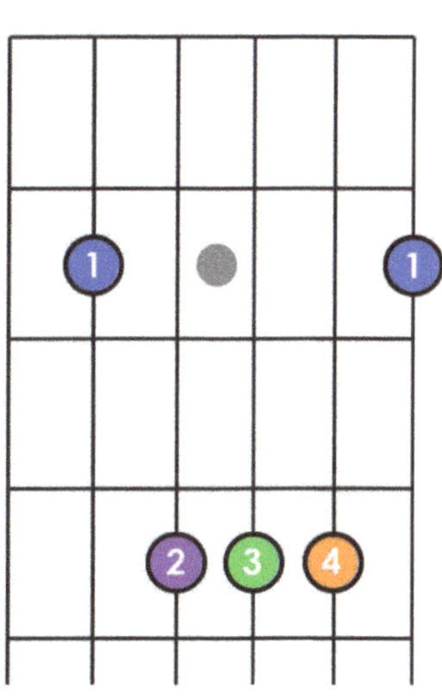

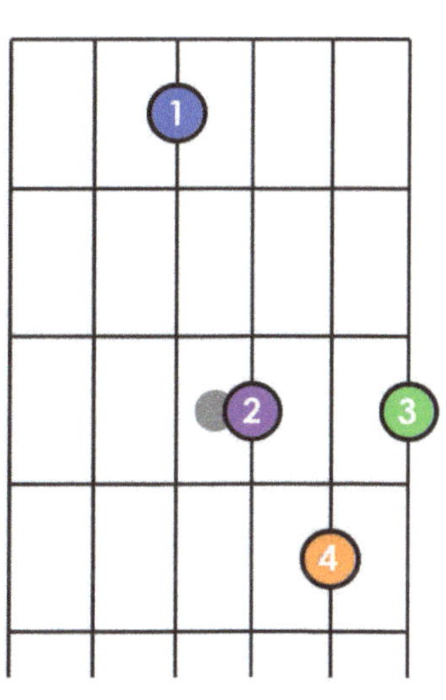

Minor Bar Chords

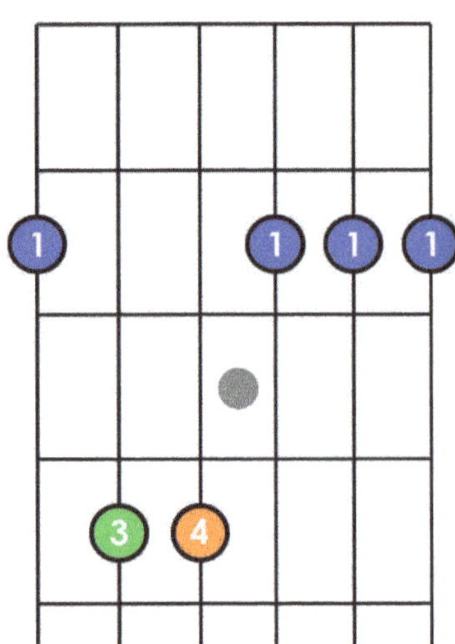

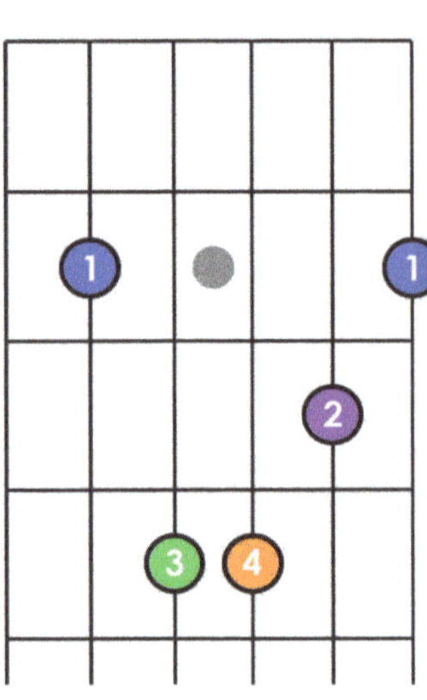

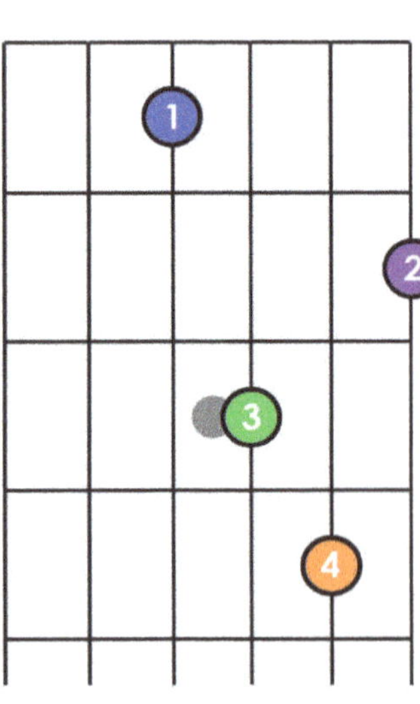

Dominant Bar Chords

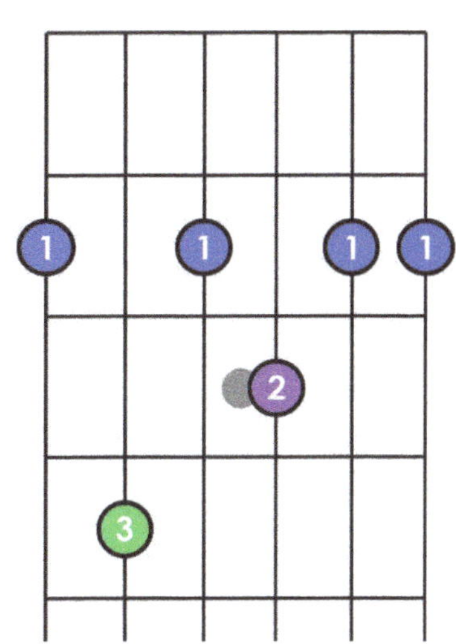

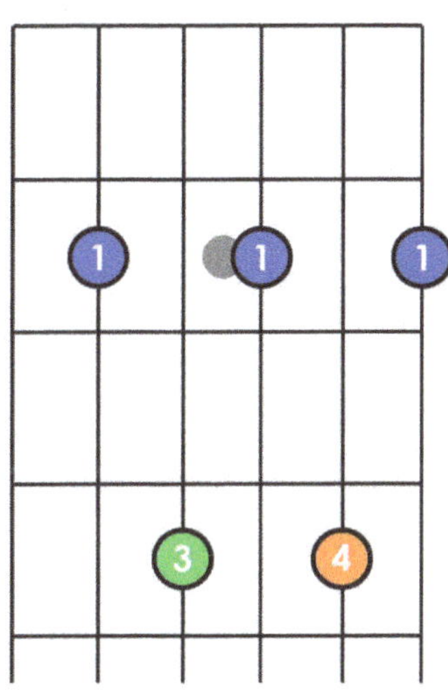

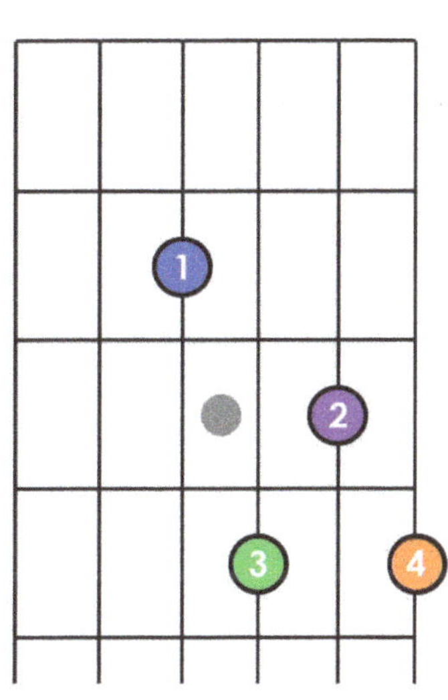

BUT WAIT... THERE'S MORE!

**Find more books, masterclasses
and practice tools at
www.jacoblamb.com**